T

THE D

WATER WITCHING

First Edition 1876
Charles Latimer

New Edition 2017
Edited by Tarl Warwick

1

COPYRIGHT AND DISCLAIMER

FOREWORD

This little work is a fine example of dowsing folklore; while the author explicitly states a belief in the concept and his own use of the same, much of the content is secondary in form and comes from various other sources, where dowsing is spoken of variously as a spiritual idea, a physical science, and a delusional hoax. It was originally written as a long essay, not apparently a booklet at all, and was released because of "public interest." This makes sense, given its era of manufacture- dowsing was in vogue at the time to a great degree.

The essential process of dowsing takes two basic stereotypical forms; Latimers' dowsing is very much like the older tradition, wherein a Y shaped piece of wood is deployed, usually to find water (the more famous use especially in cinema) but also mineral deposits, notably gold or silver. In the more modern era dowsing is also used to "close" energetic lines and often involves small copper prongs which is thought to lead to various medical benefits; proponents claim that doing this can ward off ailment or cure the medical problems being experienced at any given time. Some of this is new age in form; the original dowsing practice was not indicated as beneficial in that manner.

This edition of "The Divining Rod" has been edited for format and some archaic word usage cleaned up for modern standards. Care has been taken to retain all original intent and meaning.

PREFACE

My Essay on the "Divining Rod," (*Vulgus*, "Water-Witching,") having proved interesting to a number of my friends, I have concluded to give it to the public, with the hope that some useful practical results may be derived from it. I have no apology to make for presenting this subject in a serious light.

I regard it as one strictly in the domain of science, and, therefore, worthy of the consideration of scientific men. I have no fear of ridicule, knowing for myself and "not for another," that what is here presented is the truth.

To those who seek absolute truth, I need not recommend a reading of these pages. To those who merely live by science, drawing their sustenance from it as from the "convenient cow," as Goethe says, I will simply say, imprison yourselves, gentlemen, in your shell; the world will move quite as well without you.

I add a number of notes from various sources to which I had not access before writing my own experience.

THE DIVINING ROD

ABOUT "WATER-WITCHING."
(WHAT I KNOW.)

I have always observed that when any novelty is presented for the consideration of man, which is not readily proven by already well known scientific laws, or which may not be demonstrated by the knowledge and power of most persons, it is found extremely difficult, if not impossible, to gain the attention of the devotee of science.

Whether, indeed, it be from lack of interest, from incredulity, or from the fear of ridicule, or from any other cause, we look with distrust upon anything which is not in harmony with our preconceived ideas or theories, and we are apt to raise the cry of humbug or superstition, and reject, with a contemptuous assumption of superiority as unbelievers, propositions which properly put up the test might prove of value to mankind. Happily for us a wise Providence has not ordained that all minds shall plow in a single furrow of the great field of knowledge. Some, therefore, believe nothing but what they see, and frequently doubt the evidence of their own senses.

Others believe everything they see and nearly everything they hear, and seize with too great credulity upon every new thing presented to them. There are others who disbelieve nothing that is presented to them, however apocryphal, without full and impartial investigation, aided not by testimony alone, but by actual demonstration. Again, there are men who are afraid to investigate, lest the world should call them visionary; these are always prepared to apologize for examining anything outside the mere routine of their special science. But the most frequent error of mankind is to doubt and ridicule, without investigation, everything which is not commonly received. To such I would cite the pungent words of Solomon: "He that answereth a matter before he heareth it, it is a folly and a shame unto him."

I feel that I am speaking to those, who always listen with interest to every proposition, and are willing to examine it, until its demonstration is clear and its hidden mysteries revealed, and never pronounce anything a superstition or an imposture, until from patient research they have a right, through their own experimental knowledge, to utter a verdict. But, lest there should be among us one of these doubting Thomases or disbelieving cynics, I would appeal to him with the history of the two Spanish students. These two young gentlemen, while traveling from Penaflor to Salamanca, stopped at a spring to quench their thirst, and whilst seated upon the ground near the fountain observed something like a tombstone, level with the water; engraved on the stone were these words: "Here lies interred the soul of Pedro Garcia." The youngest of the students, a thoughtless fellow, said, laughing loudly: "What a joke. Here lies interred the soul! Who ever heard of a soul being buried? who can tell me the author of so ridiculous an epitaph?" The other, a reflective, judicious youth, said to himself: "There is some mystery here, and I intend to solve it before I leave this spot." Letting his companion depart, without losing a moment's time, he took out his knife, cut around the stone, dug under it a little, and there found buried a purse containing one hundred ducats, with these words in Latin inscribed upon it: "I declare thee my heir, whomsoe'er thou art, who hast had the genius to understand the meaning of the inscription; but I charge thee to use this money better than I used it."

Now to the point. The subject to which I am about to call your attention- that of finding water by means of the "divining rod"- is one of those which in modern times is classed among mere superstitions, and as such unworthy of serious consideration by sensible people. I think I have it in my power to demonstrate to you, principally from my own personal experiences- the relation of which I beg you to accept as strictly accurate- that this is an error on the part of the over-wise skeptics of our progressive epoch.

Worcester's dictionary gives the following definition of the "divining rod"; "A forked branch, usually of hazel, said to be useful to discern mines and water."

"Witch-hazel- a tall shrub of eastern North America, remarkable for blossoming late in the autumn."

Another authority gives the following: "Divining rod- A hazel twig cut in the form of a Y, by the aid of which certain persons (meaning, of course, sorcerers like myself,) called 'dowsers,' pretend to be able to discover water or mineral veins. The rod is held in a peculiar manner, and the 'dowsers' walk backward and forward over the ground to be tried. As soon as he crosses or approaches a metallic vein or aqueous spring the twig turns toward it with a slow, rotary motion. This superstition has not yet died out, and 'dowsers' are yet common in remote parts of England, France and Germany."

Now, one can easily see that this writer is one of those who apologize for seeming to believe a thing of the kind by calling it "a superstition not yet died out."

Here is another definition: "Divining rod- A forked branch, usually of hazel, by which it has been pretended that minerals and water may be discovered in the earth. The rod, if slowly carried along in suspension, dipping and pointing downwards, it is affirmed when brought over the spot, where the concealed mine or spring is situated. The form, the material and the mode of using the divining rod of the modern miners and water finders seem to be superstitions of comparative recent introduction. Many persons with some pretensions to science have been believers in the powers ascribed to the 'divining rod.' "

Here we have another case of the apologetic historian. He dared not say that he believed it, even though he had seen it. Why? Simply because there was no scientific fact or theory upon which he could base his belief- so he was afraid even to say what he believed, lest people who read his encyclopedia might say he was visionary.

I read somewhere, a long time ago, that this superstition was also rife in the eleventh century. Now, like the young students above cited, someone among you may exclaim, "Who will inform me who can be the author of this ridiculous superstition?" I wish I could tell you; I am sorry I can not, but I should not wonder if he lived before the days of Moses, the first 'dowser' on record. When oil was discovered in this country many of us believed that there was at last 'something new under the sun.' We have only to turn to the Scriptures to learn that Job was in the oil and dairy business a few thousand years before Oil City sprung up under our wondering eyes. Job has always been supposed to refer to some great miracle when he says, in the 29th chapter of his book, "I washed my steps with butter and the rock poured me out rivers of oil; the young men saw me and hid themselves."

Also, in Deuteronomy, we read, chapter 32, verse 13, "And he made him to suck honey out of the rock, and oil out of the flinty rock." Now, we have these marvels repeating themselves daily; and I think it no very far fetched idea to assume that the "divining rod" was used in the discovery of these precious deposits. I am myself acquainted with a gentleman who has lately successfully located two oil wells by this magic (so-called) process. In fact, who knows but that the first knowledge of the " divining rod" was a revelation, and that Moses not only understood the art, but taught it to the Children of Israel, from whence the supposed superstition has spread.

When Moses found the water at Meribeh-Rephidim and Meribeh-Kadesh, in the wilderness of Zin, he had received the Almighty' s command: "Go before the people and take with thee the elders of Israel, and thy rod wherewith thou smotest the river; take it in thine hand and go. Behold, I will stand before thee upon the rock in Horeb, and thou shalt smite the rock, and then shall come water out of it, that the people may drink; and Moses did so in the sight of the elders of Israel."

In the 20th chapter of Numbers we read of a similar miracle occurring three years afterward- "And Moses took the rod from before the Lord as he commanded him, and said. Hear, now, ye rebels, must we fetch water out of this rock. And Moses lifted up his hand and with his rod smote the rock twice, and the water came out abudantly and the congregation drank and their beasts also."

Now in the 21st chapter of Numbers we find these verses: "And from thence they went to Beer, that is, the well whereof the Lord spake unto Moses. Gather the people together and I will give them water. Then sang Israel this song- Spring up, O, well! sing ye unto it. The princes digged the well, the nobles of the people digged it, by the direction of the lawgiver, with their staves." This shows that the lawgiver pointed out the places for them to dig, and the people made the wells.

There is nothing like faithful searching if you wish to find; so I advise you to look back also as far as Confucius, and then come down to the old monk, Roger Bacon, and it would not surprise me if you should ascertain that those old wise heads had gone even farther than your humble servant into the mysteries of the divining rod. But I will not quote from these ancients; I will only look back a short hundred years. In Sir David Brewster's

THE DIVINING ROD

Philosophy you will find that he says that there is no doubt that the presence of water can be detected by the divining rod, although it can not be demonstrated by any known science. It was this last paragraph which I stumbled upon many years ago, that first brought me to a practical knowledge of this phenomenon. I read it, and being on a visit in Raymond, Miss., I went to Judge, of that place, a scholar and a man of good sense, whom I took for granted had not failed to gather in, among his great stores of learning, something about the topic which had struck me so forcibly. I was not mistaken; the old gentleman told me that he had not only heard a good deal about this matter, but possessed, himself, the power of finding water, offering to show me how he proceeded. Soon after we went, accompanied by my brother, Dr. L., to a spot where there was a well known under-ground stream.

The Judge cut three forked branches from a peach tree, each took one and we marched over the spot indicated, holding our rods according to the approved style of the 'dowser' proper. At a certain point the switches in the hands of the Judge and myself went down simultaneously; the effect was very apparent; but my brother, in whose hands there was no movement, mercilessly ridiculed the whole proceeding; neither the Judge nor I being at all disconcerted by his skeptical derision of our scientific research. I could not be shaken from faith in my actual, absolute experience, and was fully convinced that there was a mysterious power, beyond my ken, that turned the switch. I pondered over the matter, and resolved that at some future day I would examine more closely into it.

This, to me, decisive epoch finally came after a great number of trials, always with satisfactory results as to the bare fact that water could be traced or discovered. That the switch did turn in my hand readily was undoubtedly true- the agency which moved it was the mystery.

THE DIVINING ROD

I knew that electricity had broad shoulders, and had always carried the weight of every unexplained phenomenon. I said this switch turns by electric force. Having evolved my theory, I set out to sustain it, by experiment. Upon inquiry, I found that not only could water be discovered, but it was asserted that minerals as readily answered to the call of the magic rod; and, indeed, that even their depth beneath the earth' s surface might be computed.

Granting this to be true, I concluded that I had not only a philosophical but a mathematical problem to solve. I, however, never met any one having any information on. this latter point, nor in my readings did I find any allusion to the possibility of ascertaining the depth below the surface of any concealed stream or mineral. On the contrary, I found the general impression to be that the whole thing was a superstition of ignorant minds. The doubters frequently met me, and with some show of reason, with this personal argument: "I cannot believe this thing, because the switch does not turn in my hand." It is quite true that every hand does not have the power of giving the motion to the switch; but this does not disprove the fact of its turning. I have heard that the evidence of one man who heard a bell is worth that of a dozen who did not hear it. The testimony is, therefore, to my mind, clearly in favor of the 'dowsers.' All men are not the same conductors of electricity. I have known persons who could light the gas by running across the floor, rubbing their feet upon the carpet, and pointing a finger at the jet. I never saw this done, but I have no doubt that there are many who can do it, and also many who cannot.

Now, although the switch may not turn in the hands of all, this is no proof that the current producing the movement does not pass through the persons just the same- the effect is only less perceptible in some, than in others. I had made a very large number of experiments, from time to time, before I had an opportunity to make one which satisfied me that I was on the right track. I had in these experiments exploded the superstition of the "witch-hazel," and learned that peach, apple, willow, dogwood, beech, maple, iron, steel, copper- in fact, that even an old barrel hoop possessed all of its virtues, and so concluded that after all this relic of the necromancer's art of former days was a very simple matter, if we could but find the clue to it. A few years ago it happened that I wanted to get water at a place called Coloma, upon the Chicago, Michigan Lake Shore Railroad, of which I was then chief engineer. I concluded to test my electric theory here. I found that it was necessary to dig a well upon the depot grounds- the point was to see if I could find water where I needed a tank.

I took a switch and found water near the desired spot; then, with my theory in view, I made a second experiment. I bought four ink bottles, I adjusted them to a pair of wooden sandals, which I fastened to my feet. Thus insulated, I walked over the ground, my switch in hand, but, as I had anticipated, there was no movement- the diviner's rod was powerless. I therefore assume that I am right in ascribing the phenomenon to electricity. I continued my experiments, having yet the mathematical point unsettled. Upon walking over the ground again and again, I found that the switch commenced always to turn at the same places, equally (or nearly) distant from a center, and kept gradually turning until it pointed directly downward. To assure myself, I repeated this experiment many times, and arrived at the conclusion that the switch commenced to turn at an angle of forty-five degrees from the edge of the water, and that the distance from my hand to the water would be measured by the distance from the point where the switch commenced to turn to the point of absolute turn-down, and so it seems to be. The following diagram will show more clearly my meaning:

THE DIVINING ROD

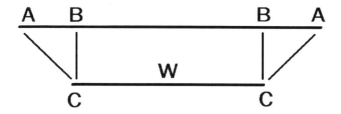

A B, B A is the surface of the earth; W, a stream or pool of water below the surface. Walking along toward A B the switch begins to move at A, and turns down at B; the angles BAC and BCA being equal, the distance from A to B is equal to BC.

Measure the distance, therefore, from the point of commencement of turning to the point of turn-down, and you have the depth from your hand to the water. I have verified this over many water-courses, upon bridges, etc., and I am satisfied it is correct, at least for the latitude in which my experiments were made. Upon this basis I made my first estimate of the depth of the water at Coloma, and gave it as from twenty-five to thirty feet. I employed an experienced well borer and had a two and one-half inch pipe driven into the ground at the exact point my switch indicated, and found water at twenty seven feet exactly. I had the pipe driven down forty feet, and found that I had thirteen feet of water in it. I then had a windmill erected and a large tank. Up to the time of my leaving the road, the engines were supplied with the water, which, besides, proved to be of excellent quality for drinking.

My well borer, who was a doubting Thomas, said he believed that he could get water at the same depth anywhere. Fortunately for my theory, a neighboring store-keeper tried the doubter and failed to get water under fifty-nine feet. Subsequent to the satisfactory experiment at Coloma it happened that on one occasion, when I was traveling west on the Hannibal & St. Joseph Railroad, that I was introduced to a gentleman engaged in building a road, who related to me that during its construction the engineers had made use of drive wells as they moved rapidly along.

As the water question was always one of interest to me, our conversation drifted, naturally, to "water-witching." The gentleman said that all of his knowledge on this subject had been obtained from his brother- a young man employed by Horace Creeley on his farm at Chappaqua. Mr. Greeley had sent for him from hearing of him as extremely intelligent and thrifty as a farm hand. It happened while the young man was at Chappaqua that a well was needed, and the question of "water-witching" came up.

The young man said that his belief was, that if one man could find water, so could another- whereupon he took a forked switch and, walking about, found that the magic wand turned down over a rock. He had a blast of powder put in at the point, the smoke of which hardly cleared away, revealed a spring of water. Here is simply a repetition of the smiting of the rock. In my own experience I have a similar instance: I was assistant superintendent at Highlands, on the Vandalia line. Mr. ___, then chief engineer, had, previous to my arrival, caused a well of ten feet diameter and forty feet depth to be dug and w ailed up with brick, but the supply of water was so small that it could be pumped out in a few minutes. A hole had then been drilled sixteen feet to the rock, which was conglomerate, of very great hardness, with no better results. The well was therefore abandoned.

If I had seen Mr. ___, I should have advised penetrating the rock, but I did not meet him, and did not wish to interfere with the work. Mr. Koepfle, the owner of the land upon which the well was located, arrived just at that time from Switzerland,

and I soon became acquainted with him. He came into my office one day and said: :Mr. Latimer, do you not think there is water under that ground?" I replied, "Yes, I thought so." "Did you ever hear of 'water-witching'?" he then asked. I said "Yes." "Can you tell where water is?" Upon my affirmative answer he requested me to go down and try a switch. I did so and found that it turned down in a number of places about the well. Mr. Koepfle came to me again to say that there was a 'dowser' in the neighborhood and to ask me what I thought of his employing him. I advised him to try the skill of this man by all means. I was not present at the trial, but a short time afterward Mr. K. came to me in great excitement to tell me that the man said there was a subterranean lake at that very point. Among other things, he told me that the wand in this case was a bit of whalebone- an item I treasured for future consideration. Mr. K had already commenced another well in a marsh about half a mile west of the first. Mr. Koepfle asked my advice as to what he should do. I replied, "I cannot take any action in the matter officially, but if you will take it upon yourself to bore through that rock and pay the expense of it, I think that no objection can be made to it, and I believe that you will get plenty of water- in which case, I am sure you will not lose your money."

"But where can I get a man?" urged Mr. Koepfle.

"Try Mr. ___'s man. I think he will be glad to get rid of the expense," I said. Mr. K. came soon after with the man and agreed, by my advice, to give him $7.50 per day for his own work and that of his man with the drills. In five days the rock was smitten through with a three inch drill, and the water immediately rushed up to a point above the natural surface of the ground, only held by the railroad bank- which surrounded the well- and there remained. I am not aware that he ever knew that his excellent well water was provided for him by the magic power of a morsel of whalebone and a peach twig.

THE DIVINING ROD

Upon one occasion, at a farm of one of my connections, the water gave out in the well, (seventeen feet deep,) which had for years supplied a large number of cattle. In the first place I ordered the well to be cleaned out, for it was very dirty; but there was no improvement. It was then decided to dig another. I found a place about ten feet north of the old well, where I judged there was a small stream, and repeatedly estimated the depth to it by my rule, and came to the conclusion that it was between ten and twelve feet. I was rather astonished at this, for the water, it may be observed, was seventeen feet deep in the old well. However the well was begun. I asked the digger at what depth water ought to be found; he said at seventeen feet, but I made this a test case, and said, "You will find water here between ten and twelve feet, but if I should have to say precisely, I should say at ten feet."

Water was found at exactly ten feet, and stood at that point after the well was finished. A peculiar test occurred at Toulon, Illinois. I was talking on the subject with a friend, a lawyer of that place, one dark night at about nine o'clock. He asked, "Can you tell how deep it is to the water in the well in this hotel yard?" I answered at once, "Yes," but said, "it is rather dark, and I know nothing about the yard or the position of the well." However I went out and started at the kitchen door, only asking upon which side of the house I should seek. I traced the stream from the kitchen door, passing back and forth rapidly until I found the well about forty feet from the kitchen and near the barn. When I came to the well I said, "This stream passes five feet from the well and does not go directly into it." I then made some examination with the rod, and pronounced the depth to the water to be fourteen feet, which was found by measurement to be correct.

I will add, that I was never before in the hotel yard, did not know where the well was located, and the night was exceedingly dark. The next morning, while paying my bill, the

16

landlord said, "You probably do not know how close was your calculation last night. I had that well dug myself, and we went down forty feet without finding water. Before giving it up the digger had himself lowered into the well, listening as he went to hear the sound of some stream. At fourteen feet he heard water, and boring in laterally five feet, where you said the stream was, he found a plentiful supply, filling the well with twenty-three feet of water."

Another experience. One day at Wyoming, Ill., a friend said to me, "I must introduce you to our 'water-witch,' " who proved to be a gentleman named ___, a banker of the place. After some conversation with him, we agreed to try an experiment together and compare experiences generally. I asked first, "What do you use?"

"Willow, hazel or peach- perhaps any green twig would do as well; but I only employ those three." "What would you say to an old barrel hoop?" I asked. "Oh, that would not do at all; there must be sap in the wood." We each took our rod and went forth, I holding mine in my hands, whilst my companion held one end of his in his teeth, the other in both hands. I asked what he meant by that mode of holding the switch. He replied, "That is my way; there is no chance for presumption or pretense in it some persons can make the switch turn and be deceived." I observed that our switches moved at the same moment, mine turning down, his sideways; but in every case we agreed, and thus traced a number of streams. I tried his plan, but it would not answer, while his switch moved held in either way. In discussing the matter, I asked his theory, which he declined to give, but which I divined by a question he asked, namely; "Did you ever see a switch turn for stagnant water?" I said, "Yes." "Well," he responded, "I never did, and the rod will not turn over stagnant water for me." "Now," said I, "I understand your theory; it is that the friction of running waters underground produces an electric current which causes the switch to turn." He admitted that I was right. "Now," I said, "I propose to explode two of your notions at once. In the first place, let us get an old barrel hoop." I found one, which we divided. I then went with him across the railroad track, which at that place runs north and south. The rod turned down for both of us at once, in this case he used the rod in his hand. "Now, you see," I said, "that the rail represents stagnant water, and you find that a dry twig or stick is as good as a green one." I then obtained a piece of copper wire from the telegraph office and gave him. He walked across the track with it in his mouth and hands, and in every case the rod turned to the south for him. In finding water the rod always turned for him in the direction the stream ran. I found he knew nothing about estimating the depth beneath the surface. He remarked that he had fancied that he knew much of the subject, but that a man must 'live and learn.' I went with him to his bank, where we threw down a rod of iron on the floor, and with our switches found the movement to be the same at every trial. Again, we placed a silver coin on the floor, with the same result- trying several times with his hand on my arm. I told him that I meant to invent an instrument for finding water and estimating its depth.

A few months ago I received a letter from him, asking after my proposed invention. This gentleman gave me a curious confirmation of my experiment at Coloma. He related that a few days previous a friend had been out with him to try if the switch would turn in his hand. It did readily; but after dinner he found, upon a second trial, that there was no movement. This mystery was soon explained by the discovery that our neophyte was standing in his India-rubber shoes. Another important test I made at the Naval Academy, at Annapolis, a few years ago. I went there to look at Sir David Thompson's Electrometer, to ascertain if it could give me a clue to something which might guide me in the invention of the instrument in question. I could discover nothing from it, or from the most delicate galvanometer.

THE DIVINING ROD

One of the professors, however, asked me to give them a test. I called for a piece of iron wire, walked a few feet, put my foot down and said "There is something immediately under here."

The board was taken up and disclosed the gas pipe. I asked if they were satisfied. "You are a man of quick perceptions and might have noticed the direction of the pipe," was the answer. "Are you willing to be blindfolded?" I consented and succeeded repeatedly in locating the pipe, and what is more, in indicating other points of attraction to the rod, where all said that my experiment had failed, but which proved as full a confirmation of my theory as the lead pipe. These points were those where the iron columns supporting the building touched the ceiling underneath.

Upon one occasion, I visited Professor Henry, of the Smithsonian Institute, and presented the subject to him. The professor took notes in a book, and asked for a test. I gave him several by locating the gas and water pipes. We then sat down and the professor remarked: "This is all personal influence." Of course, the question is none the less important or curious on this account, and I was a little nettled at the summary disposal of the matter. I therefore replied: "Professor Henry, you scientific men are always behindhand in discoveries, because you will not investigate, and it is left to those not well versed in the laws of science to ferret out mysteries and lay them bare. I present you two things, Professor- first, I find, by insulating myself that there is no motion of the rod, which proves electricity; second, I show that the motion begins at a certain point- an angle of forty-five degrees from the concealed water or metal, and the rod turns down directly over it; thus physical science and mathematics disprove your theory." I will say that my remarks moved the professor, who then showed a very decided interest and asked me to come and spend the following morning with him.

THE DIVINING ROD

Unfortunately, my departure from the city deprived me of the proposed interview. I have had many other experiences, but the relation of them would demand more time than it is expedient to give to them at present. I would add that I have observed in my experiments that the smallest underground stream affects the rod in my hand in the same degree as the cataract of Niagara itself, and that the presence of a stove, a bar of iron, or any other metal- a water or gas pipe, causes it to turn with the same movement as a large mineral deposit; but it is my belief that there is a hidden mode of distinguishing between them all, outside of all questions of personal influence. We know that in what we call the dark age of the world, all unexplained phenomena were referred to personal witchcraft. We, as yet, know little of the many phenomena of electricity, and in the midst of our own intelligent population we find, that, to very many, the working of the electric telegraph itself is ascribed to superhuman agency. Only a few days ago an intelligent telegraph operator and his wife, at Horican, thought the spirits were communicating with him through the wires because they heard the air "Home, Sweet Home" in their vibrations- not knowing that he was receiving a musical message from the newly invented telephone, played at Chicago many miles distant.

I have desired to show that the use of the "divining rod" is at least as old as the Mosaic dispensation; that the knowledge or tradition of its use has been understood, to some extent, by certain "wise" men in all ages, and that in the present age- one of inquiry and research- many have a knowledge of it and make use of it to their own advantage; that there is no superstition in the matter, but that it is governed by fixed laws; that it requires only intelligent research and earnest investigation to understand them thoroughly, and, finally, to arrive at results of the greatest practical benefit to mankind. When we understand that the earth is a great electric ball, giving and receiving electricity with the nature of the conductors which transport or absorb the various currents, we may arrive at more comprehensive and correct theories about natural phenomena.

I picked up, a few days since, a periodical containing an admirable article on the Electric Telegraph, describing most vividly the motion of the currents, and I make use of the words of the writer to illustrate how it is possible to bring this subject to a scientific test:

"The observer, whom we have supposed capable of seeing electricity, would find that the whole surface of the earth, the atmosphere and probably the fathomless space beyond, were teeming with manifestations of the electric force. Every chemical process and every blow in nature or in art evolves it. The great process of vegetation and the reciprocal process of animal life all over the globe are accompanied by it. As incessantly as the sun's rays pass around the earth, warming every part in alternation with the cooling influences of night, great currents or fluctuations of magnetic tension, which never cease their play, circulate about the globe, and other apparently irregular currents come and go according to laws not yet understood; while the aurora borealis, flaming in the sky, indicates the measureless extent of this wonderful power, the existence of which the world has but begun to discover. Our observer would see that these great earth currents infinitely transcend the little artificial currents which men produce in their insulated wires, and that they constantly interfere with the latter, attracting or driving them from their work, and making them play truant, greatly to the vexation of the operators and sometimes to the entire confusion of business. If a thunder-storm passed across the country, he would see all the wires sparkling with unusual excitement. When the rain fell and water, which is a conductor, trickled along the wires and stood in drops upon the insulators, he would see the electricity of the line deserting its path and stealing off slyly, in greater or less quantities, over the wet surface of the insulators or by the wet straws or kite strings which sometimes hang across the line. Now and then he might see the free electricity of the storm overleap the barriers and take possession for the moment of some unguarded circuit, frightening operators from their posts. Such an observer would realize what it is difficult adequately to conceive, that electricity is, as has been said, the hidden force in nature, and still remains, as far as man is concerned, almost dormant. A high scientific authority has remarked, in speaking of metals, that the abundance of any object in nature, bears a proportion to its adaptation to the service of man. If this be true in general, we may expect electricity will become, one day, a familiar thing.

I conclude with a word from the wise and godly man I have before cited: "Oh that mine enemy would write a book," cried Job. Of course, he meant a book setting forth some newfangled idea which he knew would bring upon its author the whole army of cavilers. This my little book or essay may bring upon me the same legions, grown mightier with the centuries which have elapsed since Job's day. To them, I can only reply, 'Truth is mighty and will prevail.' "

From Br. Ashburner in Beichenbach's *Dynamics of Magnetism.*

However vulgar and absurd, because, perhaps, not severely exact to habitually erroneous thinkers themselves, may appear much of the knowledge floating among boors and peasants, a very remarkable proof of the importance of some of it is seen in a singular, though rude anticipation of a part of the most brilliant of Professor Faraday's discoveries on magnetism and diamagnetism by means of an instrument, the name of which has been sufficient to excite the contempt of some so-styled savants of repute. If knowledge be not in the range of the thoughts of certain severe cogitators, it is then forsooth, no knowledge at all. The unmerciful contempt which has been cast on the divining rod- virgula divina or *baguette dimnatoire*- by certain cultivators of science may be estimated by a reference to the earlier editions of a translation by Dr. Hutton, of Montucla' s improvement of Ozanam's Mathematical Recreations, a book full of most interesting matter. In the last edition of that work, however. Dr. Hutton proved himself to be, what he always was, a sincere lover of truth. Led into error at an earlier period, he was open to inquiry, and became, subsequently, convinced of facts, the existence of which he had at one time doubted. My friend, Mr. Charles Hutton Gregory, lent me a copy of the *Speculum Anni* for the year, 1828, in which he pointed out some passages relating to this matter which I cannot avoid extracting here, and premising a few observations on the instrument called the divining rod, *virgula divina*, *haculus divinatorius, baguette dimnatoire*. This has been supposed to be a branch of a tree or shrub, necessarily of a forked or letter V shape, by the assistance of which, certain gifted persons were enabled to discover mines, springs of water underground, hidden treasures, and to practice other occult doings. This, with regard to shape, is just as vulgar an error as that which supposes that a stick of any kind of wood, held in the hand, serves as well as the hazel or white thorn, for the production of the phenomena.

In the counties of Somerset, Devon and Cornwall, the facts on this subject are well known, and the practice of 'dowsing,' as it is called, has been cultivated time out of mind. In France, the men of scientific pursuit have for the most part ridiculed the use of the baguette, notwithstanding abundant evidence in various parts of the country being extant of the success which has attended the practice of the *sorciers*. The Baron Von Reichenbach has established facts regarding the emanation of lights from graves which are quite as remarkable as the proofs of emanations taking place from metals or from running water. Now that the Baron' s researches and the concurrent testimony of the cultivators of mesmeric science have established that certain individuals are more susceptible of magnetic impressions than others, it will not be pronounced impossible that subterranean running water may influence some persons and not others.

In different classes the sensitive powers are known to vary greatly as they do indeed among those of the same species. "But," it has been asked, "granting that emanations from subterranean waters may powerfully effect certain persons, what connection is there between this impression and the motion or rotation of the hazel rod which is held in the person' s hand or laid over his fingers?" What! is it fact that the hazel rod or white thorn moves or rotates in the hands of a person of a certain impressionability, when that person passes over any ground underneath his footsteps on which there happens to be a metallic lode or a subterranean stream of water which we call a spring? I have been informed by highly respectable persons, who have in the West of England, witnessed the facts, that under these circumstances a hazel or a white thorn rod does rotate and does move and occasionally dips with so energetic a force that on one occasion the bark of a fresh hazel rod was stripped from the stick and left in the grasp of the operator's hand.

The following extracts will further illustrate the subject: "Although the effects or motion of the divining rod, when in the proximity of springs, has been and is to this day considered by most philosophers a mere illusion, yet I think the following brief observations relating to the subject, and which was communicated to Dr. Hutton by a lady of rank, with the account of her subsequent experiments performed before him, his family and a number of friends, (as given in the Doctor's translation of Montucla's edition of Ozanam's Recreations), must convince the most incredulous that in the hands of some persons in certain situations the baguette is forcibly acted on by some unknown, invisible cause. Notwithstanding the incredulity expressed by Montucla relative to the indication of springs by the baguette or divining rod, there appears to exist such evidences of the reality of that motion as it seems next to be impossible to be questioned. This evidence was brought about in the following manner. Soon after the publication of the former edition of the Recreations, the editor received by the post the following well written pseudonymous letter on the subject of this problem. The letter in question is dated Feb. 10, 1805, and, as with the whole correspondence it would be too long for our limits, I shall select such parts only as are immediately essential to a right understanding of the subject.

The lady observes, 'In the year 1772, (I was then nineteen), I passed six months at Aix en Provence. I there heard the popular story of one of the fountains in that city having been discovered by a boy who always expressed an aversion for, passing one particular spot, crying out each time there was water. This was held by myself and by the family I was with, in utter contempt. In the course of the spring the family went to pass a week at the Chateau d'Ansonis, situated a few miles to the north of the Durance, a tract of country very mountainous and where water was ill supplied. We found the Marquis d'Ansonis busied in erecting what may be termed a miniature aqueduct to convey a spring the distance of half a league, or nearly as much, to his chateau, which spring he asserted had been found out by a peasant, who made the discovery of water his occupation in that country, and maintained himself by it, and was known by the appellation of L'Homme a la Baguette. This account was received with unbelief almost amounting to derision. The Marquis, piqued with being discredited, sent for the man and requested we would witness the experiment.

A large party of French and English accordingly attended. The man was quite a peasant In manners and appearance : he produced some twigs cut from a hazel, of different sizes and strength, only they were forked branches, and hazel was preferred as forking more equally than most other trees, but it was not requisite that the angle should be of any particular number of degrees.

He held the ends of the twigs between each forefinger and thumb, with the vertex pointing downwards. Standing where there was no water, the baguette remained motionless. Walking gradually to the spot where the spring was under ground, the twig was sensibly affected; and, as he approached the spot, began to turn round; that is, the vertex raised itself and turned towards his body, and continued to turn till the point was vertical; it then descended outwards, and continued to turn, describing a circle as long as he remained standing over the spring, or till one or both the branches were broken by the twisting, the ends being firmly grasped by the fingers and thumbs, and the hands kept stationary, so that the rotary motion must, of course, twist them.

After seeing him do this repeatedly, the whole party tried the baguette in succession, but without effect. I chanced to be the last. No sooner did I hold the twig as directed than it began to move as with him, which startled me so much, that I dropped it and felt considerably agitated. I was, however, induced to resume the experiment, and the effect was perfect. I was then told it was no very unusual thing, many having that faculty- which, from what has since come to my knowledge, I have reason to believe is true. On my return to England I forbore to let this faculty (or whatever you may term it) be known, fearing to become the topic of conversation or discussion. But two years afterwards, being on a visit to a nobleman's house, Kimbolton, Huntingdonshire, and his lady lamenting that she was disappointed of building a dairy house on a spot she particularly wished, because there was no water to be found- a supply she looked on as essential- under promise of secrecy I told her I would endeavor to find a spring. I accordingly procured some hazel twigs, and in the presence of herself and husband, walked over the ground proposed, till the twig turned with considerable force. A stake was immediately driven into the ground to mark the spot, which was not very distant from where they had before sunk. They then took me to another and distant building in the park, and desired me to try there. I found the baguette turn very strong, so that it soon twisted and broke. The gentleman persisted that there was no water there, unless at a great depth, the foundation being very deep (a considerable stone cellar) and that no water appeared when they dug for it. I could only reply that I knew no more than from the baguette turning, and that I had too little experience of its powers or certainty, to answer for the truth of its indications. He then acknowledged that when that building was erected they were obliged to drive piles for the whole foundation, as they met with nothing but a quicksand. This induced him to dig in the spot I first directed. They met with a very fluent spring; the dairy was built and it is at this time supplied by it. I could give a long detail of other trials I have made, all of which have been convincing of the truth, but they would be tedious. For some years past. I have been indifferent about its becoming known, and have consequently been frequently requested to show the experiment, which has often been done to persons of high estimation for understanding and knowledge, and I believe they have all been convinced. Three people I have met with who have, on trying, found themselves possessed of the same faculty. I shall add only one more particular incident. Having once shown it to a party, we returned into the house to a room on the ground floor. I was again asked how I held the twig. Taking one in my hand, I found it turned immediately; on which an old lady, mother to the gentleman of the house, said that room was formed out of an old cloister, in which cloister was a well, simply boarded over when they made the room.

THE DIVINING ROD

L'Homme a la Baguette, from experience, could with tolerable accuracy, tell the depth at which the springs were, and their volume, from the force with which the baguette turned; I can only give a rough guess. In strong frost, I think its powers not so great. On a bridge or in a boat, I think it has no effect- the water must be underground to affect the baguette, and running through wooden pipes acts the same as a spring. I can neither make the baguette turn where there is no water, nor prevent it from turning where there is any, and I am perfectly ignorant of the cause why it turns. The only sensation I am conscious of, is, an emotion similar to that felt on being startled by sudden noise, or surprise of any kind.

I generally use a baguette about six inches from the vertex to the ends of the twigs where they are cut off. I shall most probably be in London next winter, and will (if you wish it) afford you an opportunity of making your own observations on this curious fact."

The lady arrived in London, wrote to Dr. Hutton to inform him that she proposed being in Woolwich on Friday, the 30th inst., (May, 1806,) at eleven in the forenoon. 'Accordingly,' says Dr. H., 'at the time appointed, the lady, with all her family, arrived at my house at Woolwich Common, where, after preparing the rods, etc., they walked out to the grounds, accompanied by the individuals of my own family and some friends; when Lady showed the experiment several times in different places, holding the rods, the divining rod etc., in the manner as described in her Ladyship's first letter above given. In the places where I had good reason to know that no water was to be found, the rod was always quiescent; but in other places, where I knew there was water below the surface, the rods turned slowly and regularly, in the manner above described, till the twigs twisted themselves off below the fingers, which were considerably indented by so forcibly holding the rods between them.

All the company present stood close around the lady, with all eyes intently fixed on her hands and the rods, to watch if any particular motion might be made by the fingers, but in vain; nothing of the kind was perceived, and all the company could observe no cause or reason why the rods should move in the manner they were seen to do. After the experiments were ended, every one of the company tried the rods in the same manner as they saw the lady had done, but without the least motion from any of them. And, in my family, among ourselves, we have since then several times tried if we could possibly cause the rod to turn by means of any trick, or twisting of the fingers held in the manner the lady did; but in vain, we had no power to accomplish it.'

The annexed figure represents the form and position of the rod, about six inches in length, cut off just below the joint or junction of the two twigs."

There can be no impropriety in stating now that the lady in question was the Honorable Lady Milbanke, wife of Sir Ralph Milbanke, Bart., (afterward Noel,) and mother of the present. Dowager Lady Byron, wife and widow of the great poet. A very interesting analogous statement relating to the same person will be found in the Quarterly Review for March, 1820, No. XLIV, volume 32:

"Lately, in France, the Count de Tristan has published a work on the subject, and a most interesting volume, containing two memoirs has been written By M. Thouvenel, a physician of reputation in France, who was commissioned in the year 1781, by the king, to analyze and report upon the mineral and medicinal waters of the kingdom.

The author undertakes a patient and laborious investigation, in the spirit of a philosopher, and regards his inquiries as leading to a new thread in the tangled skein of physics, which, like any fact of science, may lead to the discovery of a thousand others; a fact which may have escaped the vigilant sagacity of observers, or which may have been totally abandoned to the blind credulity of worthy soft-headed persons, or, in short, since the reign of a kind of false philosophy, the offspring of scientific pride, may have been delivered over to the presumption of men of false wisdom.

Thouvenel found a man named Bleton, whose business was that of a *sorcier,* or discoverer of springs by means of the divining rod, and upon this man he made more than six hundred observations, many of them in the presence of above one hundred and fifty persons, mostly of important stations, and very creditable from their high character, who testify to the truth of the observed phenomena. Among others, was M. Jadelet, professor of physic at Nancy, a man eminent for his abilities, who was not only a witness of these experiments, but was actually concerned in the greatest part of them. As in the case of Lady Milbanke, with Bleton an internal feeling was coincident with the movement of the rod. Whenever this man was in a place where there existed subterranean waters, he was immediately

THE DIVINING ROD

sensible of a lively impression, referable to the diaphragm, which he called his "'commotion.'" This was followed by a sense of oppression in the. Upper part of the chest; at the same time he felt a shook, with general tremor and chilliness, staggering of the legs, stiffness of the wrists, with twitchings, a concentrated pulse, which gradually diminished.

All these symptoms were more or less strong, according to the volume and depth of the water, and they were more sensibly felt when Bleton went in a direction against the subterranean current than when he followed its course. Stagnant water under ground did not affect him, nor did open sheets of water, ponds, lakes or rivers affect him. The nervous system of this man must have been susceptible, since he was more sensibly affected by change of weather and variations in the atmosphere than other persons; otherwise he appeared healthy. A severe acute disorder had absolutely at one time deprived him of the faculty of perceiving water, and his sensibility in this respect did not return until three months after his recovery, so that if he were sensitive, he could not be classed among the sick sensitive.

But however remarkable these constitutional peculiarities may have been, there was in Bleton's case a more than usual distinctness in the behavior of the divining rod. Unlike many *sorciers*, he did not grasp it closely; he did not warm it in his hands ; he did not prefer a young, hard branch, forked, newly plucked and full of sap. His custom was to place horizontally on his forefinger and thumb a rod of any kind of wood (except elder), fresh or dry, not forked, only a little curved or bent. A very straight rod failed to turn on its axis, but a bent rod turned on its axis with more or less rapidity, according to the quantity of the water and the force of the current.

Thouvenel counted from thirty-five to eighty revolutions in a minute, and always noted an exact proportion between the rotation of the rod and the convulsive motions of Bleton. If these memoirs be critically examined, it will be found that the author experimented with full care to avoid every source of fallacy. The natural motions of the rod on Bleton's fingers were backward, but as soon as he withdrew from the spring over which he stood, in any direction whatever, the rod, which instantly ceased to tarn, was subject to a new law, for at a determinate distance from the spring an action of rotation in a direction contrary to the former one took place. This was invariable, and upon measuring the distance of the spot where this retrograde phenomenon took place, from the spring, the depth could generally be found.

I pass over an account of numerous experiments made by this intelligent and careful observer, pointing out the analogies of the known phenomena of electricity and magnetism, by modifications resulting to the sensibility of Bleton, and the rotation of the rod by various ingenious electrical and magnetic trials suggested by the inventive sagacity of Thouvenel, in order to arrive at the curious anticipations of some of Professor Faraday's discoveries, by means of the sensibility of Bleton and the invariable laws which regulated the rotation of the divining rod, when the experiments were made over places where various substances have been concealed under ground. It was found that whether the trials were made in this manner, or over masses of coal, subterranean currents of water or metallic veins, the divining rod indicated a determined sphere of electric activity, and was, in fact, an electrometrical rod. 'Of all the phenomena relating to the distinction of fossil bodies,' says Thouvenel, 'acting by their electrical emanations, doubtless the most surprising is this; upon the mines of iron, of whatever kind they may be, the rods supported by the fingers of Bleton turned constantly on their axes from. behind forward, as upon the mines of coal; while upon other metallic mines, as upon other metals extracted from their mines, the rotary movement took place in the contrary direction, that is to say, from before backward. This circular movement, which never varies while Bleton is in a perpendicular position over mines or upon metals, presents revolutions as rapid and as regular as the revolutions in the contrary direction upon the mines of iron and coal.'

The constitutional effects of spasms and convulsive twitchings took place more or less in all the veins, but copper emanations excited very strong and disagreeable spasmodic symptoms, accompanied by pains about the heart, by flatulent movements in the bowels, and by abundant eructations of air. On lead, there seemed to be less unpleasant consequences, but stronger again on the mines of antimony. Having previously determined that for Bleton, on all the metals except iron, there existed a sphere of electric activity which propagated itself toward the west, a great number of experiments were made, which always had the same results. At the depth of two, three or four feet under ground were buried gold, silver, copper, tin, lead and iron. The weight of each was only from five to eight pounds. In other similar pits, pyrites of all kinds, sulfur, coal, resin, wax and lard were buried. All these different deposits were made at distances from each other in gardens or in open country, and they were so well covered over and concealed, that nothing could be perceived but private marks, to be known only by certain assistants. Over the resin, wax and lard, Bleton experienced nothing.

Over the coal, there was a decided effect, the convulsive tremor of muscle was manifest, and the rod rotated from behind forward. Over the iron, the same indications, but more energetic. A feeble impression from the sulfur, but sufficient to establish a difference between it and the two preceding; and the rod over the sulfur turned from before backward. Pyrites produced the same rotation as sulfur, and a slight tendency of the electric sphere toward the west. Gold and copper especially exhibited strongly this singular tendency of the active electric emanations. Over silver, tin and lead, also, it was more remarkable.

It extends itself more or less from the focus of the metals according to their depth and their mass. For example, in describing a circle having a radius of three or four feet from this focus, Bleton felt absolutely no action except on the line of the west. It was the same when, in proceeding from the vertical point of the focus, he successively traversed all the radii of the circle, or even if he went from all the points of the circumference to proceed to the center. In these two inverse proceedings it was always only on the radii going westward, that his person and the rods were affected by movements more or less intense, according to the kinds of metal.

It must, however, be admitted that the action of these metals presenting only the differences of greater or less in degree, either in the nervous and muscular impressions of the body or in the circular revolutions of the rods constantly moved from before backward, these differences do not yield a certain means of distinguishing the five metals one from the other. The object Thouvenel had in view was nevertheless fulfilled, for he had established the extent and the determination of a sphere of electric activity towards the west in certain metals and on sulfur which does not exist in the same manner, on iron, on coal, or on streams of water.

To give a summary then of the relations of these phenomena to those established by Professor Faraday, it may be said that over iron mines, the divining rod assumes a movement of rotation diametrically opposite to that which it exhibits over all other mines. When iron and other metals are extracted from their ores and deposited underground, the phenomenon occurs with the same distinction, that is to say, with the iron it rotates towards the north. With all other metals submitted to trial, its action is from east to west. The influence of the red metals seems to be more energetic than that of the white. But with regard to this divining rod, let one condition be remarked- the relation of the organic substance to another organic and living power of matter, to a human being in a certain susceptible state of nervous system. Thouvenel describes the symptoms which affected Bleton when he was in the sphere of metallic action, and the rod becomes the secondary part of a philosophical instrument composed of an impressionable human being and a piece of stick.

A highly respectable girl, the lady's maid of a very clever and intelligent friend of mine residing in Hertfordshire, offers, when she is mesmerized, a great many deeply interesting phenomena. She is as guileless and as good a being as can be met with, and is much beloved by her excellent and amiable mistress who has repeatedly addressed me in her case. If a piece of hazel stick or white thorn be presented to Harriet, she grasps it and sleeps mesmerically in less than a minute. The sleep is at first very intense and deep, and then the stick is held so firmly that the spasmodic state of the muscles renders it very difficult for even a powerful bystander to turn it in her hand. Harriet P's impressionability was put to a very useful purpose. Her mistress heard that she had a practice of 'dowsing' for water, and writes thus to a friend, July, 1845:

'We made a curious experiment here, some days since, with Harriet P . We have very bad water here and have long been unable to find a good spring. Mr. G. has in vain dug and dug for one. I proposed the divining rod; "for," said I, "Dr. Ashburner would not think it a foolish experiment." Harriet P. was willing, so we went forth to a field the most likely one for a spring- Mr. and Mrs. G., myself, and two friends staying here. We put Harriet to sleep with the hazel stick. She grasped it so tightly we were obliged to use the gold chain. She then held it only in one hand, and immediately began to walk, taking her own way. She went very carefully for about twenty yards, then suddenly stopped as if she had been shot. Not a word was uttered by any one. We all looked on, and were not a little surprised to see the rod slowly turn round until her hand was almost twisted backwards. It looked as if it must pain her; still no one spoke. Suddenly she exclaimed, "There! there! don't you see the stick turn? The water is here, under my hand. I see, oh, I see; let me look; don't speak to me ; I like to look."

"How deep is the water?" said Mrs. Qt., speaking to Harriet's fingers. "Oh, about three feet, I can't quite tell, but it is here." In a moment, to our astonishment, she sank down on the grass, and took the stick again in her hands.

We made a strange group around her, as we were all much astonished to see what we had come there to see. She seemed so like a witch. We marked the place, and, after a few minutes, we awoke her. In the evening she was again mesmerized to sleep, and we asked her what she saw at the spring. "Why, I saw water, water everywhere."

"Then," said I, "how do you know where the spring is?" "Oh, because it goes trinkle, trinkle, I know it is there." "Why did you sit down?" "Why, because I was so giddy; it seemed as if all was water but the little piece of ground I stood upon. I saw so much water, all fresh, no sea. I tried to see the sea but could not; I could not at all." Mr. Gr. caused a large hole to be dug, and just at the depth of three feet the water was found. A brick well has been constructed, and there is a good supply of excellent water. No one could doubt the action of the rod, it turned so evidently of itself in her hand. Of course, when awake, Harriet knew nothing of the circumstance.' "

So many and so various are the testimonies and the facts relating to the divining rod, that it would be tedious to recite the hundreds of respectable documents offered by those authors who have written on the subject. A work by Tardy de Montravel, printed in 1781, entitled "Memoire Physique et Medichiale sur la Baguette Divinatoire," abounds in testimonies of the truth of the same class of facts. One of the most curious works on this subject, is a little book entitled "Occult Physics, or treatise on the Divining Wand and on its utility in the discovery of springs of water, mines, concealed treasures, thieves, and escaped murderers, with principles which explain the most obscure phenomena of Nature," by L.L. de Vallemont, Ph. D. This work, embellished with plates, illustrating the different kinds of divining rods with the various modes of holding them for use, appeared at the latter part of the seventeenth century, and passed through several editions in France and Holland. It is remarkable for much curious literary and historical learning, and for able statements of the arguments which were used in the controversies rife at that period, on the realities of the facts under consideration.

It contains a curious catalog of a great number of mines discovered in France, by means of the divining rod, made out by a German mineralogist employed for the purpose by the Cardinal de Richelieu.

From Encyclopedia Americana.:

Divining Rod: A rod made with certain superstitious ceremonies, either single and curved, or with two branches like a fork, of wood, brass or other metal. The rod is held in a particular way, and if it bends towards one side, those who use the rod believe it to be an indication that there is treasure under the spot. Some publications respecting a man who, in quite recent times pretended to be able to discover water and metals under the ground by his feelings, attracted much attention.

THE DIVINING ROD

Campetti, an Italian, born at Gargnano, on Lake Garda, has attracted much attention in our time by pretending to be capable of ascertaining by his feelings the places where metals and water exist under ground. Many experiments seem to confirm his statements. The King of Bavaria sent for him in 1806, and he came to Munich, where the experiments were renewed.

These experiments were chiefly made with pendulums of sulfurous pyrites, which are said to vibrate if brought near to metals.

Rhahdomancy is the power considered by some as existing in particular individuals, partly natural and partly acquired, of discovering things hid in the earth, especially metals, ores, and bodies of water, by a change in their perceptions, and likewise the art of aiding the discovery of these substances by the use of certain instruments; for example, the divining rod.

That rhabdomancy, generally speaking, is little more than self-delusion, or intentional deception, is now the opinion of most natural philosophers and physiologists. Still it has some champions. From the most remote periods, indications are found of the art of discovering veins of ore and water concealed in the bowels of the earth, by a direct perception of their existence. The divining rod is held in the hand so that the curvature is inclined outward. If the person who holds the rod possesses the powers of rhabdomancy, and touches the metal or any other magnetic substance, or comes near them, a slow, rotatory motion of the rod ensues in different directions, according to particular circumstances; and, as in the other cases, no motion takes place without a direct or indirect contact with a living person. In the South of France and Switzerland this art is frequently made use of under the name of metalloscope (when discovering or feeling

THE DIVINING ROD

for metals,) and of hydroscope (when discovering or feeling for water).

From Chamber's Encyclopedia:

The Divining Rod: often called the Virgula Divina, the Baculus Divinatorius, the Caduceus, or Wand of Mercury, the Rod of Aaron, etc; is a forked branch, usually of hazel, sometimes of iron, or even brass or copper, by which it has been pretended that minerals and water have been discovered beneath the surface of the earth. The rod when suspended by the two prongs, sometimes between the balls of the thumbs, will distinctly indicate by a decided inclination, it is alleged, the spot over which the concealed mine or spring is situated.

Many men, even of some pretensions to scientific knowledge, have been believers in the occult power ascribed to the magic wand. Agricola, Sperlingius, and Kirchmayer, all believed in its supernatural influence. So did Richelet, the author of the Dictionary. The learned Morhoff remained in suspense, while Thouvenot and Pryce, in the latter part of the eighteenth century, gave ample records of its power.

In a work published by Dr. Herbert Mayo, in 1847 and 1851, entitled, "On the Truth Contained in Popular Superstitions," he gave some curious illustrations of the art, supposed to be possessed by one in forty of the Cornish miners. At Weilbach, in Nassau, he likewise met with one Leebold, who, he says, possessed the power, but afterwards lost it. Arthur Phippen, in 1853, published a pamphlet containing an account of two professional diviners, or 'dowsers.' One of them, named Adams, gave remarkable indications of being able to detect water underground. He not only was able to discover the particular spot where the water might be found, he could even perceive a whole line of water running underground.

THE DIVINING ROD

From Hartwings Subterranean World:

As far back as the eleventh century, the divining rod came into practice and found full credence in a superstitious age. A forked branch of hazel tree, cut during a peculiar phase of the moon, was the means employed in Germany for the discovery of buried treasures, of veins of metals, of deposits of salt, or of subterranean sources.

But the miraculous rod did not indiscriminately show its power in every hand. It was necessary to have been born in certain months, and soft and warm, or- according to modern expression- magnetic fingers were indispensable for handling it with effect. The diviner possessing these qualifications took hold of the rod by its branches so that the stem into which they united was directed upwards.

On approaching the spot where the sought for treasure lay concealed, the magical rod slowly turned towards it, until finally the stem had fully changed its position, pointed vertically downwards. To increase the solemnity of the scene, the wily conjurers generally traced magical circles, that were not to be passed, burnt strong smelling herbs and spices, and uttered powerful charms, to disarm the enmity of the evil spirits that were supposed to guard the hidden treasures.

From American Cyclopedia:

Divining Rod; The increase of knowledge has not yet expelled even from' the educated portions of the United States all faith in the magic virtues of this instrument.

There is a mystery in the hidden flow of subterranean courses of water, and in the occurrence of deposits of valuable ores, which encourage a resort to mysterious methods for discovering them. If the wise can point to no sure clue to them, the ignorant pretender does not fail to find one, which to many is all the more acceptable for its extravagant pretensions and inexplicable nature. It is stated by a writer in the "American Journal of Science," (Vol. 11, 1826,) that the divining rod has been in frequent use since the eleventh century.

A work was published in France, in 1871, detailing six hundred experiments made to ascertain the facts attributed to it, "by which is unfolded," according to this work, "their resemblance to the admirable and uniform laws of electricity and magnetism."

These sciences still continue to be appealed to in order to support in some vague way phenomena which defy other means of explication. As commonly used, the divining rod is a forked, slender stick of witch hazel; elastic twigs, however, of any sort, or even two sticks of whalebone fastened together at one end, do not appear to be rejected in the want of the hazel tree. One branch of the twig is taken in each hand between the thumb and forefinger, the two ends pointing down. Holding the stick in this position, the palms towards the face, the gifted operator passes over the surface of the ground; and whenever the upper point of the stick bends over and points downward, there he affirms the spring or metallic vein will be found.

Some even pretend to designate the distance below the surface according to the force of the movement, or according to the diameter of the circle over which the action is perceived, one rule being that the depth is half the diameter of this circle; whence, the deeper the object is, below the surface, the further is its influence exerted. It is observable that a rod so held will of necessity turn as the hands are closed more tightly upon it, though this has at first the appearance of serving to resist its motion. From the character of many who use the rod and believe

THE DIVINING ROD

in it, it is also plain that this force is exerted without any intention or consciousness on their part, and that they are themselves honestly deceived by the movement.

On putting the experiment to the test by digging, if water is found it proves the genuineness of the operation; if it is not found, something else is, to which the effect is attributed, or the water which attracted the rod is sure to be met with if the digging is only continued deep enough. Some ingenuity is therefore necessary to expose the deception. The writer above referred to succeeded in showing the absurdity of the operation by taking the 'diviners' over the same ground twice, the second time blindfolded, and each time marking the points designated by the rod. This, however, is a test to which they are not often willing to subject their art.

Some operators do not require a forked twig. There was, in 1857, and may be still, within less than one hundred miles from New York, a man who believed himself gifted in the use of the divining rod, and was occasionally sent for to go great distances, to determine the position of objects of value sunk in the lakes, of ores and of wells of water. He carried several little cylinders of tin, but what they contained was a secret. One had an attraction for iron, another for copper, a third for water, etc. He had in his hand a little rattan cane, which he used as not likely to excite the observation of those he met. Taking one of the cylinders out of his pocket he slipped the rattan into a socket in its end, and holding in his hands the other end of the stick, he set the contrivance bobbing up and down and around. That it was attracted and drawn towards any body of ore in the vicinity he was evidently convinced.

From 'Notes and Queries':

Divining Rod: Divination by the rod or wand is

mentioned in the prophecy of Ezekiel. Hosea, too, reproaches the Jews as being infected with the like superstition: "My people ask counsel at their stocks and their staff declareth unto them." Chap, IV, 12. Not only the Chaldeans used rods for divination, but almost every nation which has pretended to that science, has practiced the same method. Herodotus mentions it as a custom of the Alani, and Tacitus of the old Grermans. See Cambridge's "Scribleriad," book V, note on line 21. In the manuscript "Discourse on Witchcraft," 1705, written by Mr. John Bell, page 41, I find the following account from Theophylact on the subject of rabdomanteia or rod-divination: "They set up two staffs, and, having whispered some verses and incantations, the staffs fell by the operation of daemons. Then they considered which way each of them fell- forward or backward, to the right or left hand- and agreeably gave responses, having made use of the fall of their staffs for their signs,"

Dr. Henry, in his "History of Great Britain," tells us (II, 550), that after the Anglo-Saxons and Danes embraced the Christian religion, the clergy were commanded by the canons to preach very frequently against diviners, sorcerers, auguries, omens, charms, incantations, and all the filth of the wicked and dotages of the Gentiles."

The following is from "Epigrams, etc.," published London, 1651; Virgiula Divina:

"Some sorcerers do boast they have a rod,
Gathered with vows and sacrifice,
And (borne about) will strangely nod
To hidden treasure where it lies
Mankind is (sure) that rod divine,
For to the wealthiest (ever) they incline.'"

The earliest use made of the divining rod by the miners

THE DIVINING ROD

was for the discovery of the lode. So late as three years ago (1850), the process has been tried. The method of procedure was to cut the twig of an hazel or apple-tree of twelve months growth, into a forked shape, and to hold this by both hands in a peculiar way, walking across the land until the twig bent, which was taken as an indication of the locality of the lode. The person who generally practices this divination boasts himself to be the seventh son of a seventh son. The twig of hazel bends in his hands to the conviction of the miners that ore is present; but then the peculiar manner in which the twig is held, bringing muscular action to bear upon it, accounts for its gradual deflection, and the circumstance of the strata walked over always containing ore gives a further credit to the process of divination.

The vulgar notion still prevalent in the north of England of the hazel's tendency to a vein of lead ore, seam or stratum of coal, etc., seems to be a vestige of this rod divination.

The *virgula dimna ov haculus dimnatorius* is a forked branch in the form of a Y, cut off an hazel stick, by means whereof people have pretended to discover mines, springs, etc., underground. The method of using it is this: the person who bears it, walking very slowly over the places where he suspects mines or springs may be, the effluvia exhaling from the metals, or vapor from the water impregnating the wood, makes it dip or decline, which is the sign of a discovery. In the Living Library or *Historicall Meditations* we read: "Just as man can tell why forked sticks of hazel (rather than sticks of other trees growing upon the very same places) are fit to shew the places where the veins of gold and silver are." See Lilly's History of his Life and Times, for a curious experiment (which he confesses, however, to have failed), to discover hidden treasure by the hazel rod.

In the Gentleman's Magazine, for February, 1752, XXII, 77, we read: "M. Linnaeus, when he was upon his voyage to

THE DIVINING ROD

Scania, hearing his secretary highly extol the virtues of his divining rod, was willing to convince himself of its insufficiency, and for that purpose concealed a purse of one hundred ducats under a ranunculus which grew by itself in a meadow and bid the secretary find it if he could. The wand discovered nothing, and M. Linnaeus' s mark was soon trampled down by this company who were present; so that when M. Linnaeus went to finish the experiment by fetching the gold himself, he was utterly at a loss where to seek it. The man with the wand assisted him and pronounced that it could not lie the way they were going, but quite the contrary; so he pursued the direction of his wand and actually dag out the gold. M. Linnaeus adds, that such another experiment would make a proselyte of him." We read in the same book for November, 1751, XXI, 507: "So early as Agricola, the divining rod was in much request, and has obtained great credit for its discovery where to dig for metals and springs of water; for some years past its reputation has been on the decline, but lately it has been revived by an ingenious gentleman who, from numerous experiments, hath good reason to believe its effects to be more than imagination.

He says that hazel and willow rods, he has by experience found, will actually answer, with all persons in a good state of health, if they are used with moderation and at some distance of time, and after meals, when the operator is in good spirits. The hazel, willow and elm are all attracted by springs of water. Some persons have the virtue intermittently; the rod in their hands will attract one half hour and repel the next. The rod is attracted by all metals, coals, amber and limestone, but with different degrees of strength. The best rods are those from the hazel or nut tree, as they are pliant and tough and cut in the winter months. A shoot that terminates equally forked is to be met with two single ones of a length and size may be tied together by a thread and will answer as well as the other."

THE DIVINING ROD

In the supplement to the Athenian Oracle, p. 234, we read that "the experiment of a hazel's tendency 'to a vein' of lead ore is limited to St. John Baptist' s Eve, and that with an hazel of that same year's growth."

There is a treatise in French entitled, *La Phisique Occulte ou Traite de la Baguette Divinatoire, et de son utilite pour la, decouverte des sources d'Eau, des Minieres, de Tresors caches, des Voleurs et des Meurtriers fugitifs: par M. L. L. de Vallemont pretre et docteur en theologie;* 12 mo., Amsterdam, 1693. 464 pages.

From Brand's Popular Antiquities:

At the end of Henry Alan' s edition of Cicero's treatise *De Divinatione, and De Fate*, 1839, will be found "*Catalogus auctorum de divinatione ac fato, de oraculis, de somniis, de astrologia, de daemonibus, de magia id genus aliis.*"

With the divining rod seems connected a lusus naturae of ash tree bough resembling the litui of the Roman augurs and the Christian pastoral staff which still obtains a place, if not on this account I know not why, in the catalog of popular superstitions. Seven or eight years ago, I remember to have seen one of these, which I thought extremely beautiful and curious, in the house of an old woman at Beeralston, in Devonshire, of whom I would most gladly have purchased it; but she declined parting with it on any account, thinking it would be unlucky to do so. Mr. Grostling, in the Antiquarian Repertory, II, 164, has some observations on this subject. He thinks the lituus or staff, with the crook at one end, which the augurs of old carried as badges of their profession and instruments in the superstitious exercise of it, was not made of metal but of the substance above mentioned. Whether, says he, to call it a work of art or nature may be doubted; some were probably of the former kind; others,

THE DIVINING ROD

Hogarth, in his Analysis of Beauty, calls lusus natures found in plants of different sorts, and in one of the plates of that work gives a specimen of a very elegant one, a branch of ash. I should rather, continues he, style it a distemper or distortion of nature; for it seems the effect of a wound by some insect which, piercing to the heart of the plant with its proboscis, poisons that, while the bark remains uninjured and proceeds in its growth, but formed into various stripes, flatness and curves for the want of the support which nature designed it. The beauty, some of these arrive at, might well consecrate them to the mysterious fopperies of heathenism, and their rarity occasions imitations of them by art. The pastoral staff of the Church of Rome seems to have been formed from the vegetable litui, though the general idea is that it is an imitation of the shepherd's crook. The engravings given in the Antiquarian Repertory are of carved branches of the ash.

From Modern Magic, by M. Shele de Vere, published 1873:

The relations in which some men stand to nature are sometimes so close as to enable them to make discoveries which are impossible to others.

This is, for instance, the case with persons who feel the presence of waters or of metals. The former have, from time immemorial, generally used a wand, the so-called divining rod, which, according to Pliny, was already known to the ancient Etruscans as a means for the discovery of hidden springs. An Italian author, Amoretti, who has given special attention to this subject, states that at least every fifth man is susceptible to the influence of water and metals, but this is evidently an overestimate. In recent times many persons have been known to possess this gift of discovering hidden springs or subterranean masses of water, and these have but rarely employed an instrument.

47

THE DIVINING ROD

Catharine Beutler, of Thurgovia, in Switzerland, and Anna Maria Brugger, of the same place, were both so seriously affected by the presence of water that they fell into violent nervous excitement when they happened to cross places beneath which, large quantities were concealed, and became perfectly exhausted. In France, a class of men, called sourciers, have for ages possessed this instinctive power of perceiving the presence of water, and others, like the famous Abbe Paramelle, have cultivated the natural gift till they were finally enabled, by a mere cursory examination of a landscape, to ascertain whether large masses of water were hidden anywhere, and to indicate the precise spots where they might be found.

Why water and metals should almost always go hand in hand in connection with this peculiar gift, is not quite clear; but the staff of Hermes, having probably the form of the divining rod was always represented as giving the command over the treasures of the earth, and the Orphic Hymn (v. 527,) calls it, hence, the "golden rod, producing wealth and happiness." On the other hand, the *Aquae Virga*, the nymph of springs, had also a divining rod in her hand, and Numa, inspired by a water-nymph, established the worship of waters in connection of that of the dead. For here, also, riches and death seem to have entered into a strange alliance.

Del Rio, in his *Disquisitiones Magicae*, mentions thus the Kahuri of Spain- the lynx-eyed, as he translates the name- who were able, on Wednesdays and Saturdays, to discover all the veins of metals or of water beneath the surface, all hidden treasures and corpses in their coffins. There is at least one instance recorded, where a person possessed the power to see even more than the Rahuris. This was a Portuguese lady, Pedegache, who first attracted attention by being able to discover subterranean springs and their connections, a gift which brought her great honors after she had informed the king of all the

48

THE DIVINING ROD

various supplies of water which were hidden near a palace which he was about to build. Shafts were sunk according to her directions, and not only water was found but also various soils and stones which she had foretold would have to be pierced.

She also seems to have cultivated her talent, for we hear of her next being able to discover treasures, even valuable antique statues in the interior of houses, and finally she reached such a degree of intuition that she saw the inner parts of the human body, and pointed out their diseases and defects.

The divining rod, originally a twig of willow or hazel, is often made of metal, and the impression prevails that in such cases an electric current arising from the subterranean water or metals enters the diviner's body by the feet, passes through him, and finally affects the two branches of the rod, which represent opposite poles. It is certain that when the electric current is interrupted, the power of the divining rod is suspended.

From Notes and Queries:

Perhaps, like many of your correspondents, I had imagined that the supposed properties of the divining rod had been a discovery recently made, either by the great American artist, Mr. Barnum, or by one of *Dii Minores* of this country. To my mortification, however, I find that it is "as old as the hills," or at least contemporaneous with the Sortes Virgiliangae, *et id genus omne*. I have before me the works of Mr. Abraham Cowley, in two vols. 12 mo., London, 1681, and in one of his Pindarique Odes, addressed to Mr. Hobs, I find the following lines:

> To walk in ruins like vain ghosts, we love,
> And with fond divining wands,
> We search among the dead

THE DIVINING ROD

For treasures buried.

And to these lines is added the following note; "Virgula Divina, or divining wand, is a two-forked branch of a hazel tree which is used for the finding out either of veins or hidden treasures of gold or silver, and being carried about bends downwards (or rather is said to do so,) when it comes to the place where they lie."

In the first edition of his Mathematical Recreations, Dr. Hutton laughed at the divining rod. In the interval between that and the second edition a lady made him change his note, by using one before him, at Woolwich. Hutton had the courage to publish the account of the experiment in his second edition, after the account he had previously given. By a letter from Hutton to Bruce, printed in the memoir of the former which the latter wrote, it appears that the lady was Lady Milbanke.

"A Cornish lady informs me that the Cornish miners to this day use the divining rod." However the pretended effect of the divining rod may be attributed to knavery and credulity by philosophers who will not take the trouble of witnessing and investigating the operation, any one who will pay a visit to the Mendip Hills, in Somersetshire, and the country around their base, may have abundant proof of the efficacy of it. Its success has been very strikingly proved along the range of the Pennard Hills, also, to the south of the Mendip. The faculty of discovering water by means of the divining rod is not possessed by every one, for indeed there are but few who possess it in any considerable degree, or in whose hands the motion of the rod, when passing over an underground stream, is very decided, and they who have it are quite unconscious of their capability until made aware of it by experiment. I saw the operation of the rod, or rather of a fork formed by the shoots of the last year, held in the hands of the experimenter by the extremities, with the angle projecting before him. When he came over the spot beneath which the water flowed, the rod, which had before been perfectly still, writhed about with considerable force, so that the holder could not keep it in its former position, and he appealed to the bystanders to notice that he had made no motion to produce this effect, and used every effort to prevent it.

The operation was several times repeated with the same result, and each time under the close inspection of shrewd and doubting, if not incredulous observers. Forks of any kind of green wood served equally well, but those of dead wood had no effect. The experimenter had discovered water, in several instances, in the same parish (Pennard), but was perfectly unaware of his capability till he was requested by his landlord to try.

The operator had the reputation of a perfectly honest man, whose word might be safely trusted, and who was incapable of attempting to deceive any one- as indeed appeared by his open and ingenuous manner and conversation on this occasion. He was a farmer, and respected by all his neighbors. So general is the conviction of the efficacy of the divining rod in discovering both water and the ores of calameni or zinc all over the Mendip, that the people are quite astonished when any doubt is expressed about it. The late Dr. Hutton wrote against the pretension, as one of many instances of deception founded upon gross ignorance and credulity, when a lady of quality, who herself possessed the faculty, called upon him and gave him experimental proof, in the neighborhood of Woolwich, that water was discoverable by that means. This, Dr. Hutton afterwards publicly acknowledged.

After delivering my essay before the Civil Engineers' Club of the Northwest, the following letter was forwarded to me by the secretary:

THE DIVINING ROD

Brownsville, Tenk:

Gentlemen: I notice that at a meeting of your honorable club, Mr. Latimer read an essay upon the subject of the "Divining Rod," and seemed to be at a loss to know how to tell whether this rod's movements pointed to or indicated any particular substance under the earth. I am now seventy-three years of age, and have been studying and experimenting with it since twenty years of age. I am not satisfied what causes the motion of it in my hands, but by experimenting, I can tell to a certainty whether I am over any substance, either water or mineral, or whether it is sulfur, salt or any other kind of water.

I am glad that investigation in this is being made by scientific men, and hope some day it may profit man. For any information you may want, address me at Brownsville, Tennessee.

Very respectfully, Haert Sangster.

Upon receipt of this letter from Mr. Sangster, I wrote to him asking him to explain to me upon what principle he could discover the difference between metals and water, and between one kind of water and another. To this I have received the following answer, just in time to add it to this publication:

Brownsville, May 10, 1876.
Latimer, Esq., Cleveland, Ohio:

Dear Sir: Your favor of the 5th inst. is before me; also that of the 15th ult. You must excuse me for not answering the latter sooner, owing to ill health and other causes. I am glad to furnish you all the information in my power relative to the matter in question, because I would like to see it developed- as I believe it will be eventually- into a tangible, practical and useful science.

THE DIVINING ROD

The prejudice now prevailing against it will, in my opinion, ere long be dispelled. It is impossible for me, in the space of a letter, to give a full statement of my views, theory and experience on the subject of finding the locality of metals, minerals and water under the surface of the ground; but will endeavor to answer the inquiry of your first letter as concisely and explicitly as possible.

I understand fully the method of calculating the depth of water beneath the surface. What you wish to know is, after the substance is shown to exist beneath a certain point, whether it be mineral, metal or water, and the kind, character and description of each. As you are aware of the fact, the simple "forked rod" will indicate the presence of either of these. Now, to tell which of these it is, and the character of the same; if it be water, the kind of water. This is my method of testing the same, whether it be water, mineral or metal: It is on the principle of affinity- the attraction that like substances have for each other. After the rod indicates the particular spot, I take a sponge and saturate it with ordinary drinking water, either from spring or well, and put it on the top of the rod, and test it with this. If the substance beneath be water, and the same kind of that in the sponge, it will turn much stronger, and the demonstration be more active and powerful. But, if the rod should not turn at all, it will be some other substance, either mineral or metal. To test the kind of water, after I am satisfied that it is water- to discover, for instance, whether it be sulfur water, I dip my sponge in that kind of water, and test as above. If the movement of the rod be active and strong when this is done, the water below will be that species of water. If salt water, dip the sponge in that kind of water, and the result will be similar; and so on through the whole catalog of waters.

In regard to the metals. The tests are made in a similar manner. After I discover by proper tests that it is a metal, which are as follows: If it be metal or mineral, after the sponge is saturated with water, the rod will not act at all. I then put a piece of metal on the top of the rod; first, a small bit of iron. If there is no movement of the rod at the spot already indicated, it is safe to conclude that the substance is not of that nature; so I continue the experiment with different kinds of metal- lead, silver, copper, tin, gold, etc., until I find some one of these that will cause the rod to turn and operate in a manner sufficiently strong and satisfactory.

The same method pertains to the minerals. Of course, a great deal of the practical operations of these various tests, will depend upon one's discretion and judgment at the time they are made, which it is impossible to put upon paper. This is but a general outline of the system. If I can be of any further assistance to you in the investigation of this subject, do not fail to let me know of it. Would be pleased to hear from you at any and all times. Be sure and send me your pamphlet.

Yours, respectfully, Haert Sangster.

Immediately after receiving this letter, I made some experiments as follows: I took a green, forked twig, and found that over iron water-pipe, gas-pipe, and over a cistern of water, it turned down vigorously. I then took a wet rag and fastened it on top of the twig or rod. As Mr. Sangster testifies, I found it powerless over the iron water pipe and over the gas pipe, but it turned rapidly over the cistern. I put a key on the end of the rod over the wet rag; then the rod turned over both iron pipes promptly. Again, I took off the rag and put the key on the rod, and walking to the cistern, found that there was no movement. I took off the key and the rod turned instantly. I have no doubt but that he is correct as regards other metals.

THE DIVINING ROD

CONCLUSION

If any one, after the perusal of these pages, is disposed to doubt the efficacy of the divining rod, he will find it at least difficult to explain the coincidences between my experiences and those of the various persons presented in the foregoing pages- all confirming most fully conclusions reached by me, after many experiments made when quite alone. And, he must be even more eccentric than L' Homme a la Baguette, who does not find in the subject a treasure hidden, well worthy of his research.

It will be noticed that I can lay claim to no originality, or rather to no knowledge beyond that of the greater number of the parties mentioned, in regard to the fact of the discovery of minerals or waters; but, I find myself in advance in two essentials. First, I absolutely proved, by insulating myself on glass or India rubber sandals, that the electric emanations were cut off.

Secondly, that these emanations universally radiate at an angle of forty-five degrees from the horizontal, and thus the calculation of the depth below the surface, is simply the solution of a mathematical problem.

In this theory of the invariable law of electric emanations, I have received the strongest confirmation in the perusal of Baron Von Reichenbach's Dynamics of Magnetism. By numerous and varied experiments, Reichenbach proved that from metals, and especially from magnets, there is a constant emanation of electric flame upward, at an angle of forty-five degrees with the horizon.

For a more serious study of the subject, I refer the reader to the work itself, which is full of curious and well authenticated experiences.

Finally, I would paraphrase the words of my friend, the renowned Pedro Garcia: "To thee, whomsoever thou art, who mayst have the genius to investigate and the courage to face wise fools, I predict a valuable discovery, which will benefit the human race."

THE END

70165816R00033

Made in the USA
Middletown, DE
11 April 2018